History of

An Overview of the most Important People and Events in The World's Religions, Mythologies, & History of the Church

Table of Contents

Introduction

Welcome to this brief guide to the history of the world's religions! Although societies differ tremendously in terms of their customs and laws, every group of people in recorded history has practiced some kind of religion. For the purposes of this book, 'religion' is here defined as 'a set of beliefs and practices centered around the idea of, and worship of, one or more supernatural powers.' Broadly speaking, religions come in two main varieties. The first kind, comprising of monotheistic traditions (e.g. Judaism and Islam), is based around the worship of one being or god. Polytheistic religions, on the other hand, feature multiple deities. Examples of polytheism include the ancient Greek religion, which included 12 major deities and many other minor figures.

In this guide, you will be introduced to the six major world religions – Buddhism, Christianity, Hinduism, Islam, Judaism, and Sikhism. You will also gain a basic grounding in ancient Egyptian and Norse mythology plus the various Native American religions. Although these ancient legends are no longer regarded as literally true and do not form the basis of any widely-practiced religion, their impact on contemporary culture is still significant and for this reason, they are still worthy of study. Religion has been – and indeed, remains – a key motive for wars on a small and large scale, and it is vital to realize the importance many people attach to their belief systems.

In our age of ever-increasing connectivity and travel, more of us have the opportunity to meet people of other cultures. In order to create a world of peace rather than a world characterized by conflict and violent differences in opinion, we need to take the time and effort to understand how others live and what they believe. Learning about the value systems of other countries, groups and cultures is an important step forward in living in harmony. May this guide help you develop your own understanding and appreciation of religious diversity.

Polytheistic and Monotheistic Religions

Religion is that system of activities and beliefs directed toward that which is perceived to be of sacred value and transforming power.

James Livingston

Religion is a social phenomenon that is subject to the certain laws of the formation, development, and disappearance. It can be defined as a spiritual connection between one group of people with some higher, holy being, or deity. The word religion is derived from the Latin Religio, meaning 'restraint,' or Relegere which means to show respect for what is sacred. Religion is a form of social consciousness through which all the natural and social forces seem as supernatural, independent of man, nature or history. Every religion represents teaching the simple relations between nature, purpose and origin of all existing. Also, every religion implies certain forms of religious communities, as well as certain rites - rituals, performed in the holy places, and in certain institutions (churches, mosques, synagogues, temples, etc.).

The first forms of religion appear already in prehistoric period as a result of human understanding that there are many phenomena in nature, such as drought, floods, thunder, etc. that are happening on a daily basis without his will and that, as a human being, he is incapable to control or to have any kind of influence on them. This way man learned the existence of the "higher power" and, in his mind, he generated the first forms of „gods" to symbolize the unique powers that govern his existence. The man found a way, through prayers and sacrifice, to communicate and satisfy deity. One of the oldest beginnings of the ceremonial rites are the graves in a period of Homo Heidelbergensis, in Eurasia, Spain, Wales, and Croatia. Neanderthals placed their deceased in simple graves that, occasionally, would have limestone blocks placed in or on them which can, possibly, represent an archaic way of marking the graves. These practices were most likely the result of empathetic compassion towards fellow members of the tribe. In 98,000 BCE, in the area of France and Belgium, Neanderthals began to deprive of the flash of their deceased before the burial, and one of the oldest cremated humans was found near Lake Mungo in 40,000 BCE.

Additionally, by the time, burials took very important place. The oldest known animal-shaped sculpture in the world, as well as one of the oldest sculptures, in general, is the Aurignacian Lowenmensch figurine. This sculpture, even though interpreted as anthropomorphic, may as well have represented a deity.

Over time, the concept of religion took on many different meanings, and there is no generally accepted definition of religion. For some, it is just kind of feeling (emotion, experience) which is not subject to logical nor moral thinking. It is a mystical feeling of oneness with the infinite reality, experiencing the infinity, the feeling of absolute dependence, and experiencing the entire world as a God's work. On the other hand, religion is a special form of awareness of the relationship with the absolute spirit. It is an attempt to explain the origin of something that is inexplicable with a result of finding the meaning and purpose of the life.

There are three main groups of theories of religion. According to the first, religion is an invention of one (usually the ruling and privileged) group of people with a purpose to protect the privileges of that same group of individuals. According to another group theory, religion is an existential characteristic of every human being. Finally, according to the third group theory, religion is just a human tendency to the superstition that came as a result of insufficient knowledge of the true nature of things.

Nowadays religion is systematized in the primitive religions: animism and Supernaturalism and world religions: theism and systems of abstract beliefs (Taoism, Buddhism).

Organizations that occur within the religions are the church, sect, denomination, and cult.

Theism religions are polytheistic and monotheistic religions.

The main difference between polytheistic and monotheistic religion is that polytheistic religions are based on the belief of multiple gods existing, while monotheistic traditions conceive on existing only one, omnipotent, omnipresent and omniscient God, ruler of the entire universe. Polytheistic religion (Greek: poly - more, and many Theos - God) is characterized by the belief in many gods, various deities who rule the different sectors of nature and human activity. Polytheistic religions are more ritualistic and ceremonial than theoretical. Unlike monotheistic religions, polytheistic religions generally do not have a tendency to spread around the world. The most ancient religions were polytheistic (Egyptian, ancient Greek, Roman, Odin-ism, etc.). Almost all the European nations belonged to various pagan, natural, polytheistic religions in the period before Christ.

Nowadays, many of polytheistic religions are almost extinct, due to the occurrence of monotheistic, Abrahamic religions. Heavenly patriarch or monarch eventually became absolute ruler of heaven and finally there was the only one, true God, with a large entourage of angels and saints, like the court dignitaries. So monotheistic religions arise from the polytheistic religion.

Monotheistic religions (Greek: monos - one and theos - God) are characterized by the worship of one God, and that is the main difference with the polytheistic religions. Another important difference between the polytheistic and monotheistic religions is that polytheistic religions are mostly folk religions, usually limited to one clan, nation or state, while monotheistic religions are universal and supranational.

We can find some common features in all the monotheistic religions. The first common feature is the aforementioned universal, supranational character. The second - all monotheistic religions are revealed, and that means that they are established and founded by the people commonly named prophets - religious and moral reformers who, it is believed, had, each individually, interaction with a God personally. Each one of these prophets is considered as a savior of the humankind.

Finally, all monotheistic religions are eschatological, which means that all of them are based on a belief that there will be, at some point, the end of this world.

Different aspects and traditions of different religions do not exclude each other. They complement each other and lead to the conclusion that religion is a way of life. It is a life that has feelings, thoughts and actions directed toward a superior purpose, a life devoted to the to the superior creature, deity or God. All of the religions are interpreted as an ideal, imagined compensation, spiritual rejection of reality and life`s miseries that give hope and helps in everyday struggle. Typical for every religion is a faith in the afterlife. The fact of human death might be the most important when it comes to the existence of religion. The strongest human fear, fear of death, is being compensated by the religious concept of the afterlife which teaches us that death does not necessarily mean "the end" or disappearance, but rather the border between two ways of life. Faith in the afterlife made people follow the religion and believe in invisible, eternal, supernatural world, inhabited by mysterious creatures that rule the natural phenomena and human destinies.

Mythology

At the time, it was widely believed that myth is a product od primitive human consciousness and, as such, represents the prelogical moment of philosophical and scientific awareness. In such belief, the myth was considered a manifestation of primitive mentality, characteristic for archaic and traditional societies whose cultural facilities can not manifest themselves in the modern civilization.

Throughout the world, and throughout recorded human history, myths have formed an important means by which people have understood the world around them. A myth is a story that is somewhat fantastical in nature, usually contains at least one supernatural element, and is told with the intention of explaining a particular phenomenon. The term 'mythology' is used either to refer directly to myths shared by a certain group of people, or to the formal study of these stories. Each culture has its own collection of myths, some of which have been mentioned in this book.

Every culture's collection of myths usually tries to account for particular phenomena. Perhaps the most important kind of myth is the 'creation story' or 'creation myth,' which is passed down through the generations as a means of explaining how the universe came to exist in the first place. An example of this is the Norse myth of the universe arising from a sea of cosmic chaos. Another important purpose served by myths is to explain the existence of good and evil. In Egyptian mythology, good and evil became distinct, a polarized phenomenon as the result of conflict between two deities.

There are several theories as to how and why myths originated. One is the theory of elaboration or euhemerism. By this account, myths arise because storytellers in a particular culture tell and re-tell stories over and over again until the main characters are directly or indirectly granted god-like powers or importance. This early theory was put forward by

Euhermus (c.315 BCE), who argued that real human events had inspired legends about Greek gods.

Personification is another principle evoked in explaining how myths arose. Some historians and psychologist have proposed that ancient humans worshiped natural phenomena that seemed all-consuming and out of their control. For instance, not understanding how weather patterns were formed, they created deities from wind, sun, rain, and so on. In doing do, they would gain a sense of control over their environment, even if in practice this meant simply praying to, or trying to placate, the gods. According to theorist Max Muller, most myths started with poetic or allegorical descriptions of events that over time came to be taken literally.

Myths seem to bind groups of people together. In sharing a common creation myth, for example, members of a tribe, nation or religion can feel as though they have a history that unites them. Myths also serve to bind people across time. For instance, if a child grows up hearing the same creation myths that their mother, grandmother, and great-grandmother heard, this furthers their sense of taking their place among their people. Myths can also act as cautionary tales and models for proper behavior. In discussing actions taken and consequences suffered by various mythological figures, those listening to the myths are implicitly encouraged to behave in a certain way.

According to Carl Jung, similar myths tend to occur across different societies because humans all contend with the same basic set of fears and desires. For instance, they all want to understand where the universe came from, why there are good and evil in the world, and where people go after death.

The myth originated from the need for the cognition of complex natural and social phenomena. Campbell points out that traditional mythology fulfills four functions:

- Metaphysical or mystical, the compliance functions of human consciousness with living conditions;
- Cosmological function, the function of creating and establishing a particular image of the world;
- Sociological function, the function of evaluation and preserving social order;
- Psychological function, which consists in the need to align individual aspirations with the ideals of society and thus eliminates the tension in the man.

In some respects, myth precedes religion and philosophy and is, in the early stages, uncritical development of all cultures, primarily because the myth can be seen as picturesque, a fantastic story about understanding the world, and the creator of the universe. Because of this myth is recognized and determined as a lie, fantasy, collective dream or fiction, and so is opposed to scientific thought. There are different sociological understandings and interpretations of myth and mythology. Some social scientists consider that mythology is basically a primitive philosophy, and myths are stories that arise as rational attempts of a primitive man to make sense of the world in which he is located.
According to some, mythical world is nothing but a world of illusion, but an illusion which is to explain when it detects a necessity and the original self-deception from which this image comes from.

Myth can be qualified as an alternative to what is true or false. Although the myth is imaginary, it cannot be reduced to an illusion, false and misleading; it can even be false, illusory, erroneous and truthful at the same time. All the religions, even if under different names or having different rituals and traditions, share the basic idea of worshiping the world around us. The basic idea of good vs. evil is something that refers to all of the world's religions.

In primitive culture, in every religion, myth performs several functions:

- Expresses, reinforces and legitimizes the belief;
- Preserves and raises morale;
- Guaranteeing the effectiveness of ritual and contains practical experiences.

Because of this myth, it is an essential part of human civilization, and it is not a vain story, but worth the active force. It is also not an artistic conceit or intellectual explanation.

According to some theorists, myth can be divided into natural and social myths.
Natural myths relate to a specific explanation of the natural phenomena, social myths of social events.
Besides these functions and divisions, there are some of the most important characteristics that link all the myths, no matter on religion.

A panoply of gods and goddesses is very important when it comes to all the ancient polytheistic religions and myths within it. Ancient religions mostly share the common belief in multiple gods.

Very significant is the linguistic connection between the myths of different cultures. Academics have found interesting correspondence between mythological names of the gods in different cultures which suggests that Greek, Romans, and Indians originated from the same ancestors. This idea came from the conclusion that Greek god Zeus, Roman god Jupiter and Indian god Dyaus came from an older name- Dyeus Phater which means sky god or the day- father.

The most interesting myth that has uncovered a number of parallels between the different cultures might be the Flood myth. All around the world, from the ancient times, cultures have been telling the stories about the great flood and only one survivor, or a group of survivors. Babylonian Epic of Gilgamesh tells us the story of the global flood that destroyed the entire humanity leaving only one man who was in charge of saving the Earth's species by taking them on a boat. Even in case one did not read Epic of Gilgamesh he must have heard about this, we can say universal myth, very common to many other religions, and polytheistic ancient and Abrahamic. Flood myth has been described in Hindu, Greek, and Aztek mythology, as well as in sacred texts of Abrahamic religions.

The dying god is another very common theme of ancient myths. Such myths usually describe the god who returns to life after he has passed away. The motif of dying god is seen in Egyptian, Mesopotamian, and Greek culture, as well as in the Christian story of Jesus Christ.

Myth, as well as the poetry, occurs regardless of religion. However, it soon becomes content and fundamental base of the religions. Together with ceremonies and law, myth becomes supporting pillar to every religion. Mythical language is the language of the religious man who wants to express a higher, absolutely transcendent reality leaving the deity hidden, mysterious and inaccessible. Myth does not impose a "sacred, " but it refers to the "sacred" and symbolize it.

Ancient Mesopotamia

The Mesopotamians were the people, skilled artisans, and craftsmen who lived within the safety of the city walls in houses of clay brick. They were known for their magnificent palaces and temples. They have made great progress in agriculture and invented the plow wagon which the peasants used for harvesting. This invention helped the peasants to support and feed their families, militaries, and builders. There are numerous clay tablets written in Akkadian language about the epic heroes, mythical beasts, kings, and deities.

Rising above the city in layered pyramids, temples dominated over Mesopotamian cities. According to Sumerian legend, after he created one city, god founded and built five more cities on the "clean" sites, named them and made them as a center of the cult. After this, gods transmitted plans of the other cities and temples directly to the leaders. It is unknown when did religion developed in Mesopotamia but the first written records of religious practice dated to 3500 BCE. According to Mesopotamian religious beliefs, human beings were coworkers with gods. People worked with, and for gods and as a consideration, gods would hold back the forces of chaos. The gods created order out of chaos, but there was no guarantee that the forces of the chaos might not recover and overturn their strengths. Mesopotamian people, together with gods, were involved in the struggle to restrain the powers of chaos. Each one of them had their unique role in this struggle.

They believed that humans were created for the purpose to work with and for gods toward mutual benefits. In some way, Mesopotamians were slaves to their gods, yet they found their role as co-workers for they were repaid for their service. Gods would supply humans with food and drinks (beer was considered as the drink of the gods) and maintain their world. Gods were not distant entities living in heavens; they lived on earth, in the temples built by the people. In case the temple became too small or too old, Mesopotamians would build the new one on the remains. Such successive construction made the temples eventually became larger and higher, approaching the gods to the people, and people to the gods. Towering ziggurat in temple complexes was considered as literal homes of the gods. Statues of the gods were daily taken care of by the priests and priestesses. This included feeding, bathing, and even clothing. The first gods of the sky, the air, soil, and water were the supreme deities and the entire pantheon numbered more than 3,000 deities because for every aspect of human interaction with nature, gods and men together, there was one deity. Some of the most powerful gods were Marduk- patron deity of the city Babylon and Inanna- deity of love, sex, and war.

It is particularly interesting that the Lilith, originally the Sumerian goddess of desolation, in Babylon became the demon who preyed people. According to the Hebrew legend, Sumerian Lilith was actually the first woman created for Adam. Once she refused to become addicted to Adam, believing she is equal to him, she fled into the wilderness and gave birth to many demons. Jahve blamed this woman that it was she who seduced Eve and Adam to reveal the secrets of the garden in Eden.

Epic of Gilgamesh, the great king, is one of the oldest stories in the world. It is written on a dozen plates. The first half is devoted to the glorification of Gilgamesh, while the second part is telling the story about his quest to find a key for immortality which becomes his obsession. Many of themes of this story we ding in Homer's epic works as well as in the stories of the Old Testament. The main topic is the problem of human mortality.

Mesopotamian mythology is filled with dark forces; its view of the afterlife is very different from the views of other religions. The life of the common man was marked by hard work, while the religion did not give any hope of salvation that would be expected at the end of his lifetime. Torn between underground demonic forces that have threatened him at every step and pleasing the gods that watched his every move, he spent his life working in humility, knowing that after the death he will spend time in infinite standing in the dark halls of the underworld. Comparing the elements of Mesopotamian and Ancient Egyptian religion, we find many similarities; in some segments, they are almost identical. Since those two religions mutually permeate, it is easy to conclude that they are pulling together the roots from one 'parareligion "or are in the course of its history due to the geographical closeness gradually elements of one switch to another.

Egyptian Mythology

The ancient Egyptians made use of a number of stories as a means of understanding the world around them. Their accounts of creation, gods, goddesses and symbolism helped them understand a variety of natural phenomena around them. The ancient Egyptians saw the world as a collection of recurring patterns, and their myths addressed not only the original creation of the world but also the cycles seen in nature.

Egyptian mythology is based on totemism - the belief in the sacred animals. It is characterized by the gods with human bodies and animal heads, provided that there are exceptions. One of the major parts of ancient Egyptian religion is the belief in the afterlife, as evidenced by a large number of tombs found, among which are the largest pyramids, then a large number of mummies, statues, and many deities associated with the afterlife. Most gods have the ankh, the holy sign of life.

The ancient Egyptians made deities of everything – the sun, animals, the desert, the sky, and the weather. They created, and worshiped, many gods. Some gods took on human form, some were depicted as having animal bodies, and some were a mixture of the two. In addition, the same god often went by different names. For example, the deity Ra was also known as 'The Sun God.' He was depicted in Egyptian art as having a human body but the head of a hawk.

Egyptian religion was localized, meaning that various regions had their own myths and gods. However, it is fair to say that some gods were widely recognized. These included Ra (the sun god), Shu (god of the sky and offspring of Ra), Tefnut (another of Ra's children and sister-wife of Shu, goddess of rain), Osiris (grandson of Ra, god of nature and principle judge of character in the afterlife), and Hathor (goddess of love and women, shown in Egyptian artwork as possessing the head of a cow). All Egyptian Pharaohs were also worshiped as gods.

The Egyptians made reference to a creation myth in explaining how the earth came into being and why it contains good and evil. According to tradition, at the beginning of time, there was nothing except a state of chaos known as Nun. One day, the sun god Ra came from the waters and gave birth to his two children, Tefnut and Shu. His children then created Geb (the earth god) and Nut (the sky goddess).

Humanity was created from Ra's tears. However, as Ra became older and weaker, the human race began to work against him and conspire to bring about his downfall. When he found out, he ordered the goddess Hathor to kill off humankind, which she did until only a small percentage of the population remained. Before humanity could be wiped out altogether, Ra granted them a pardon. He ordered Shu to rule in his place, and he took up residence far away in the heavens.

Geb and Nut married, defying Ra. Shu, the air god, was ordered to separate them and did so successfully. Nut was pregnant, but Ra decreed that she could not give birth to her baby at any time during the year. Thoth, the god of learning, managed to help her by securing five extra days for the Egyptian calendar, enabling Nut's children to be born. Osiris, Horus, Set, Isis, and Nepthys were born in due course. Set and Osiris became the incarnations of evil and good respectively. According to ancient Egyptian religion, this tale accounts for the existence of both states in the world.

There is extensive mythology around the fights between Osiris and Set. In brief, Osiris ruled Egypt successfully until he left to bring similar prosperity to other parts of the world. Whilst he was gone, his wife Isis continued his reign. However, his evil brother Set plotted to bring about his downfall. When Osiris returned, he was captured and killed. Years of turbulence followed until finally Isis and Horus, her son, were able to defeat Set and revive Osiris. Horus went on to father four sons who, it was believed, represented the lineage from which all of

Egypt's Pharaohs were descended.

Egyptian religion was similar to Mesopotamian for they also believed that human beings are co- workers with the gods to maintain the order. However, the principle of harmony was the most important in Egyptian life, as well as in the afterlife, and their religion was integrated into every aspect of their existence. Their religion was a combination of magic, science, medicine, spiritualism, mythology, etc. The gods were friends with human beings, providing them the perfect land to live in and eternal home to enjoy once they die. This is probably to the most important difference between Egyptian and Mesopotamian religion. Egyptians strongly believed in the afterlife. Their afterlife was the Field of Reeds. It was a mirror of the life on earth. Egyptians saw earthly existence just as one part of an eternal journey. They were very concerned about passing from this life to the next phase so much that they created pyramids, temples and funerary inscriptions (Egyptian Book of Dead) in order to help the soul`s passage.

The Egyptians worshiped gods and offered them sacrifices. They considered them the masters of the world. They believed in a thousand gods, except for the period of Amarna. By order of the Pharaoh Akhenaton, all the temples were closed and the new city - Amarna was built. In Amarna, people worshiped Aton - solar disk. During the invasion of Greeks, Thoth was associated with Hermes. During the Roman Empire, Egyptians were introduced to Christianity and temples were closed. Romans issued an order to ban the worshiping of pagan gods.

Ancient Greek Mythology

Ancient Greek religion represents all religious beliefs, cults, and rituals of the population in between 2100 and 1900 BCE which settled the southern area of the Balkan Peninsula, as well as islands in the Aegean Sea. Immigrants had, together with the natives who happened to be there, accomplished the most complex pre-Christian religion of Europe.
Ancient Greek religion had an influence on the understanding of the various peoples who inhabited the Mediterranean and the Black Sea coast, especially those living in the Apennines. As Christianity became one of the dominant religions, many characters from Greek mythology have emerged as important factors of that religion, or saints. This big influence of Greek religion can be explained by its humanism, as well as its ability to assimilate other religions.

Ancient Greek religion may be reconstructed on the basis of the literary, historical, mythological and archeological sources.

Literature represents the most reliable source. Almost all sources, from Homer to Julian the Apostate contain mythological and religious components. Archaeological research has enabled the detailed study of their shrines and objects used in rituals. Greek fine art is mainly related to religion and myths. Thanks to all this, we succeeded to examine even local cults and religion, except the secret, mystical cults, because their participants were bound to silence.

The earliest phase of this religion is linked to the Middle Bronze Age (1900-1550 BCE)
We can observe history of Greek religion through four phases:

Homeric or geometric period (of about 1100th-50th BCE)

This period is called Homeric because we can mostly learn about it from Homer and Hesiod's poems. It was the period of immigration and the final stabilization of the Greek tribes.

Homer created in his work the world of gods and heroes, who are primarily described to satisfy the aristocracy. This world is different from the one in later epochs, mostly because of the fact that it has no room for the irrational and mystical. There are some connections between previous Mycenaean period and this period. For example, they took many deities from Mycenaean such as Zeus, Poseidon, and Apollo. Under the influence of Eastern religions, they established the pantheon of twelve Olimp gods. The basic characteristic of the gods in this period was anthropomorphism. The gods are subject to feelings, injuries, and have other disadvantages. They are not omnipotent and omnipresent. Even Zeus, the supreme god, must comply with the will of Moira, or fate. People are fully subordinate to the will of the gods and depend on their mood. Homer`s poems indicate that, at this period, cult of the dead was not developed. Instead, it emphasizes the idea that souls of the dead are residing in the Kingdom of the Dead, ruled by Hades and Persephone. However, archaeological findings suggest otherwise; during this period the dead were buried with food and drink which gives us the idea of continuing the life in the grave.

Unlike Homer, Hesiod introduces the dimension of time in the static world of the gods creates the history of the world from the very beginning. He systematized mythological material and introduced the gods who were unknown to Homer, such as Hestia, Prometheus, and Pandora. That is how the myth of the shift of the ruler of the world, from Uranus, over Chron, to Zeus and his posterity, was created.

Archaic period (from 50th to 500th BCE)

During this period, we can see two religious movements: Dionysian-Orphic and Apollonius. The first was the cult of the god Dionysus, who is perhaps more established in the Mycenaean. Members of this cult were mostly women, so-called maenads. Maenads were practicing sparagmos / dismembering the wild animal / and eating raw meat with the aim of becoming one with the god, Dionysus. The cult of the god Apollo developed as a response Dionysian-Orphic cult. This cult is different from the previous one, as called for reason and order. This period begins with the first Greek colony or polis. Each polis had its own patron deity, which was perfect for the flourishing of local cults, but also Greek shrines, deities, and cults. This period is characterized by a special construction of temples that were built on the Acropolis and Agora, or in the city center, as a stand-alone facility. The temples were dedicated to the gods and represented their home. An important novelty is the introduction of a cult of hero. Hero and his heroic acts constituted the legendary history of the polis.

Classical period (from 500th to 338th BCE)

Greek philosophy, in this period, attempted to explain many phenomena, which were attributed to the myth or the divine forces, explain as natural. Philosophers such as Anaximander and Xenophanes and many other, believed that religion and myth were nothing but deception. On the other hand, the myth and official religion were very accepted, especially after 650 BCE. The victory over the Persians had the consequence that many of local gods raised to the rank Panhellenic deities, especially those who have "helped" the Greeks to defeat the enemy. This way, Akkadian god Pan was widely accepted in Athens because, it was believed, that he helped the Greeks at the Battle of Marathon. Although the government took over the care of religious ceremonies, the people were still living the old religion that characterized by mysticism and archaic magical rituals. The reason was the pessimism and resignation in people because they had to obey the gods that governed everything, even their destinies. Conflicts between Greek cities in the second half of the fifth-century BCE culminated during the Peloponnesian War, which led to the religious crisis. This was also due to the great tragedians, especially Euripides. At the end of the century, and during the following, elite of Greek society moved away from traditional religion to an abstract religiosity or atheism. As a result, between ordinary people, emerged many cults with, even more deities. The final dissolution of religion in this period happened after the conquers of the Alexander the Great. His death also led to the end of this period.

Hellenistic-Roman period (from 338 BCE to the end of the fourth century)

During the Hellenistic- Roman period, philosophers continued to derogate the traditional gods and myths. They held that myths were exaggerated stories describing the real events and that their actors were ordinary people, not deities. Meantime, while gods were losing their supernatural powers, the same powers were very often attributed to the ordinary mortals. Since the period of the Alexander the Great, it became a common practice to raise the ruler to the level of deity. Therefore, from the traditional Pantheon, only those deities that were suitable for emerging opportunities were "revived." This is the reason why the members of the dynasty of Ptolemy and Seleucid enjoyed divine honors.

Greek Gods

The ancient Greeks devised a rich mythology containing many accounts of gods, goddesses, and heroes. Although now widely recognized as works of great fiction, they were held up as true accounts by many Greeks living at the time. The most famous and influential gods are known as the Twelve Olympians, so-called because they were said to live on Mount Olympus, home of the deities. There is some dispute over whether Hestia or Dionysus should be considered the twelfth deity, and so brief descriptions of both are included in this section.

Zeus ruled over all the other gods. According to Greek myth, he led the struggle against the Titans, in which the Greek Gods prevailed. Zeus is the God of the sky, order, and justice. He was often depicted holding a thunderbolt and is also associated with oak trees, scales, and eagles.

Hera was the most senior of the female deities and was the goddess of family and marriage. She was married to – and was also the sister of – Zeus. Her related symbols included peacocks, crows, and cuckoos. According to Greek myth, she often tried to exact revenge on Zeus' lovers and the children they bore him.

Poseidon was the god of earthquakes, all the seas and related events such as tidal waves. He was often shown surrounded by dolphins and depicted as carrying a trident. He was the brother of Zeus and Hades (ruler of the underworld).

Demeter was the goddess of nature, agriculture, fertility, and the changes of seasons. Her symbols were related to agriculture and included wheat, poppies, and pigs.

Athena was a goddess associated with higher intellectual functions such as intelligence, crafts, science, and strategy in warfare. She was a daughter of Zeus, and according to legend emerged from his head a full-grown woman dressed in battle regalia.

Apollo was a son of Zeus and twin brother of Artemis. He was associated with the arts, including music and poetry. He was also the god of medicine. The ancient Greeks regarded him a source of creative inspiration, light, and prophecy. His symbols include swans, lyres, and mice.

Artemis was Apollo's twin sister and another of Zeus' daughters. She was the goddess of hunting, animals, the moon, virginity, and the moon. The snake, bear, and bow and arrow are among her symbols.

Ares was the god of war, battle, and violence. He was often shown alongside boars, dogs, and serpents. In line with his reputation, another of his symbols is the sword and shield. Greek myth states that he was strongly disliked by the other deities aside from Aphrodite.

Aphrodite was the goddess of beauty and love. Often depicted with roses, doves, and apples, she was commonly believed to be a daughter of Zeus. Although she was married to Hephaestus, she was not faithful to him and embarked on many affairs. One of her lovers was Ares.

Hephaestus was a master blacksmith and considered the god of fires and of the forge. His symbols included anvils, fire, and tongs. He was a son of Hera, possibly fathered by Zeus. He was husband to Aphrodite and was known for being unusually faithful by the normal standards of behavior seen among the male deities.

Hermes was a messenger, and god of commerce. He was also a deity associated with eloquent speech, thieves, and streets. His symbols included winged sandals, a stork, and a tortoise – it was said that he invented a musical instrument using a tortoise shell. He was the product of a union between Zeus and a nymph called Maia.

Hestia was the goddess of family, hearth, and home. Although she was said to be among the original twelve Olympians, over time she appears to have been displaced in some retellings of the myths by Dionysus.

Dionysus was the god of celebrations, alcohol, and happiness. He was also associated with the performing arts. His symbols included a cup, a tiger, and grapevine. He was the youngest of the gods, and the only one who had a human mother – he was the son of Zeus and Princess Ariadne of Creta.

Ancient Roman Religion

Since the Romans had immigrated their primary gods with them from Greece, they followed the same pattern as that of Greece. However, as soon the Roman had established their religion and it was connected to the state's welfare, they enforced that they would not welcome any foreign gods into their religion. Romans had a very practical attitude to religion, and it was not based on any central belief. Their religion was based on a mixture of many rituals, superstitions, and traditions, collected over the years. In the ancient Rome, religion was not as much as a spiritual experience but more as a contract between people and deities who controlled people's existence and well-being. This way, Roman religion was based on the principle "I give that you might give." Priests of the Roman religion were only the members of the elite classes, and it was impossible to separate the religion from the state. Religion did not depend on faith or dogma, but it depended on the correct practice of prayer, rituals, and sacrifice. Religious tolerance during this period was not an issue and one could, as an individual, practice some of the mystery religions that offered salvation in the afterlife as well as take part in public religion. Concerning the rise of the city, Roman mythological tradition is very rich in myths and for the earliest period it is almost impossible to distinguish history and myth. Romans believed that heavens were ruled by the immortal gods either gods of the upper heavens, gods of the underworld, or deities between those two. They believed that many of these deities favored Rome which is the reason the Roman state had a broad network of cults. Roman most powerful of all gods was Jupiter. Roman Jupiter was same as Greek Zeus king of the gods.

Some of the other important to mention gods of Roman period are:

- Juno (Greek Hera) - goddess of marriage,
- Neptune (Greek Poseidon) God of the Sea,

- Saturn (Greek Cronos) Father of Zeus / Jupiter
- Venus (Greek Aphrodite) Goddess of Love
- Pluto (Greek Hades) God of the Underworld
- Apollo kept the same name as in Greece – God of Music and Medicine
- Athena (Greek Minerva) Goddess of Wisdom
- Mars (Greek Ares) God of War
- Cupid (Eros) God of Love

Even the most skeptical members of the Roman intellectual elite, such as Cicero, recognized the necessity of religion as a form of maintaining social order in spite of the distinct elements of the irrational.

Religion had a major role in later political conflicts and civil wars, and all the political events had to be justified by religion. However, the practice of traditional religion remained as one of the foundations of the Rome, and its development and success. The era of the Christian hegemony in Rome started when Emperor Constantine converted to Christianity. In 391. Under Theodosius I, Christianity became the state religion of Rome, in spite of all the other rituals and practicing. Starting with the 4th century, diverse religious practices around the empire were condemned as pagan and, over time, absorbed or suppressed.

Norse Mythology

Norse mythology has its origins in the pagan religions of ancient Scandinavian people – those living in Norway, Denmark and Sweden – although it continued to be spread even after the official religion of these countries was changed to Christianity. It comprises a set of stories centered around heroes and deities. These representations have been preserved in manuscripts, oral traditions, and artwork. Oral traditions were passed down in the Old Norse language, which originated in the Middle Ages and formed the foundations of contemporary Scandinavian languages. Iceland is considered to be the origin of many of the oldest texts describing Norse mythology.

A key element of Norse mythology are the gods, their actions, and their relationships with humans as well as other mythical races. Thor was the most powerful and popular god in the Viking age. He was described as carrying a hammer, which he would use to defeat enemies of both the gods and the human race. Odin is another god given a great deal of attention within Norse mythology. He carries a spear, is accompanied by ravens and wolves, and seeks out new knowledge. According to myth, he hung himself from a tree in the act of noble sacrifice so that he could obtain knowledge of the alphabet. He then decided to grant this knowledge to humanity, so that they could access written language.

Odin is also associated with death and the afterlife. He rules over Valhalla, which according to Viking lore, was the resting place of warriors who died in battle. Odin is married to Frigg, a goddess who is capable of foretelling the future (although she does not disclose this information), and he has a son named Baldr. According to Norse mythology, Baldr had a series of dreams in which he was dying. Shortly after, he was killed by Loki (a mischievous shape-shifting figure) and is forced to reside in a place known as Hel.

Although Odin is the god perhaps most commonly linked with death, he cannot claim all who pass on from the earthly plane for himself. He shares them with the goddess Freyja, who chooses her half of the dead from battlefields. Her brother, Freyr, is a god frequently linked with sexuality, pleasure, and agriculture. Other deities include Bragi, Fenrir, and Gefjon. Mythical races such as dwarves, elves and Valkyries also occur frequently in Norse mythology.

Norse creation mythology is based on the belief that there are nine worlds, all centered around a giant cosmological tree known as Yggdrasil. Asgard is the name given to the realm in which the gods live, whereas humans occupy Midgard. Norse myths often describe journeys made between the realms, as enacted by gods, humans and assorted other forms of being. The first two human beings, Ask and Embla, were supposedly created from pieces of floating wood that were made animated by the three gods who found them.

There is debate as to whether time is represented as cyclical or linear, and myths surrounding the afterlife are also not completely clear. The goddess Hel rules over a realm of the same name, and humans may reside there after death. Those who die in battle may be spirited away by Valkyries to live with Odin in Valhalla, which is represented as a large hall-like place. Gefjon, a goddess, is believed to attend the death of any virgin who passes on from the human world. There are also allusions to the possibility of reincarnation within some of the myths.

The concept of the Norse myth is quite similar in basic structure and concepts. Most of the other ancient religious groups used myth to understand the world around them. However, Greek and Norse myths, with their great meanings are considered to be the most important mythologies of the world. The Greeks and Nords, even though from two very different groups had a lot of basic ideas that were similar. They had a huge number of myths which they used to explain everything that was confusing them or did not make sense to them.

Both, Greeks and Norse believed in only one ruler of the gods and man. Greek god was Zeus and Norse god was Odin. Both of them had wives who did not have as much power as their husbands but yet again Hera (Zeus`s wife ) and Frigg (Odin` s wife) had much more power than any other god.

Each of these mythologies had the certain deities such as god of love, sea, underworld, war, etc. Norse and Greeks also had the same concept of the idea of fate and had three of these gods who were females. Both, Greeks and Norse believed that their lives were predetermined and that they can not influence on their destiny. The main difference between Greek and Norse mythologies is the mindset and personality of the stories, but this can be explained and justified by the major differences of climate between these two countries. Greece was, at one point, considered the greatest country of their time, while Norse had a difficult time due to extreme drops of temperature and barely any sunlight.

Ancient China

Religion in ancient China developed around 4500 BCE in the Yangshao Culture, long before Buddha came to China. People of China worshiped nature which, eventually, developed into religion with concepts of "wealth" or "fortune." Early structure of belief in ancient China was a mixture of animism and mythology which is evidenced on the ceramics found at the Neolithic area called Banpo Village. Designs on the ceramics include images of animals and dragons. Besides ceramics, more than 250 tombs, containing grave goods, were found. This led us to the conclusion that even in ancient times, Chinese people believed in life after death, as well as in the concept of rebirth.

Based on the grave goods that were found, scientists believe that ancient Chinese people in this period worship women and female deities who were a dominant figure in representing benevolence. While the Yangshao Culture was matrilineal, the next recorded, Quijia Culture that has inhibited the Upper Yellow River Valley was patriarchal. At this period people worshiped one, the supreme god, who was a king of many other deities. This king of the Gods got his name in Shang Dynasty-Shangti.

Shangti had the main role in all the important matters, so people were asked not to "bother "him too much with sacrifice. At this period, besides Shangti, there were over 200 gods. The early gods were spirits of the place known as Tudi Gong. Chinese people strongly believed in ghosts who were the spirits of deceased that had not been properly buried as they should be, or had some other reason the be attached to the earth. Besides spirits and Shangti, Nuwa, goddess of humankind was considered to be half a woman, half a dragon. It was believed that Nuwa brought people to life and learned them how to reproduce. Fuxi was the god of fire and teacher. He gave the fire to people similar to Greek Prometheus and taught them how to cook food and keep warm. Fuxi was considered to be Nuwa`s friend and who was helping her to teach the humans how to survive. The Zou Dynasty developed the concept of the Mandate od Heaven. Confucianism and Taoism were both influenced by ancient belief systems. Both, Confucianism and Taoism continued the ancient practices of ancestor worship. During this period, Shangti was replaced with the idea of heaven (Tian). Tian was a paradise where the dead rested eternally in peace.

I Ching

The I Ching, also known as the Classic of Changes, is an ancient Chinese text and divination manual that underlies a number of Chinese thought systems and religions such as Confucianism.It is thought to have originated from the period 750-1000 BCE and represents the culmination of thousands of years of Chinese wisdom from various sages. Essentially, the I Ching is a book comprised of symbols, imagery, advice and poetry that invites the reader to seek out solutions and guidance based on tosses of three coins (or more traditionally, 50 yarrow stalks). Its origin is sufficiently ancient and obscure that no-one can say with any certainty who wrote it.

The I Ching lists 64 'situations.' Each situation is represented by a collection of six lines, which can be broken or unbroken. Broken lines are taken to symbolize 'yin' (dark, calm, feminine energy) whilst unbroken lines symbolize 'yang' (active, light, masculine energy). To use the I Ching as an oracle, a reader needs to discover which hexagram is applicable to their situation. They can then turn to the hexagram in question and read the accompanying text.

To select the correct hexagram, a set of three coins are commonly used. The individual wishing to consult the I Ching thinks of a question to which they would like an answer whilst tossing the coins six times, once for each line of the hexagram. The first coin toss dictates the bottom line, the sixth toss the top line. Each coin toss dictates whether the line is broken or intact. When tossing the coins, tails gives a value of 2 and heads a value of 3. An even number (e.g. 2 heads and 1 tails) dictates a broken or yin line, whereas an odd number (e.g. 1 heads and 2 tails) dictates that an unbroken or yang line be drawn. However, a throw that yields all heads or all tails is considered to be a 'changing' line, and must, therefore, be changed to a yin or yang respectively when drawing up the final hexagram.Each hexagram is considered to represent a situation common to all humanity. Therefore, people of all cultures can use the I Ching.

Yin and yang are considered to be the two complementary forces seen throughout nature. They are in balance throughout the universe – active and passive, masculine and feminine. A healthy mind and body have a balance of both. The philosophy of the I Ching is simple – we can make predictions based on our knowledge of what has gone before, and the observable fluctuations between yin and yang. For instance, the changing seasons are thought to be the result of regular changes in yin and yang energies. However, this applies to human nature as well – our moods fluctuate and based on this principle, users of I Ching argue that we can attempt to predict future events based on I Ching readings.

Each of the 64 hexagrams makes reference to a particular state or prediction that makes use of the broken or unbroken nature of each line. For example, if the bottom line within a hexagram is broken, this is interpreted as indicating a fundamental weakness of some kind that must be addressed if a satisfactory outcome is to be achieved.

Traditionally, none of the hexagrams are considered 'bad' or 'good.' Rather, they are perceived as useful clues and hints for the reader, offering guidance as to how they ought to handle a particular situation. The reader must apply their maturity in determining how any particular hexagram applies to their current situation and then act accordingly in an ethical manner.

Hinduism

Hinduism is the world`s oldest organized religion, and third largest religion of the world. The most important difference between Hinduism which can not be sorted into any belief system and Abrahamic religions is that Hinduism does not have a single founder, nor a single system of morality. Hinduism also does not have central religious authority, nor the concept of the prophet. Even though Hinduism in a strict sense of the word did not exist before the modern time, Hindu traditions are ancient and embrace many traditions. However, Hinduism`s history is firmly linked with the social and political development. We classify the main historical periods of Hinduism into:

- ***Before 2000 BCE***

This is a period of the Indus Valley Civilization which had established their base on the river Indus, the present day of Pakistan. Nowadays, we do not have may recordings about religion in this period but it seems that the ancient people in the Indus Valley did have temple rituals and ritual bathing, as well as the animal sacrifice. Later, Hinduism and early Indus Valley civilizations may have some connections when it comes to these rituals and sacrifices, but these features are also common to many other ancient religions.

- ***Vedic Period (1500- 500 BCE)***

The Early Vedic period was focused on the sacrifice and sharing the sacrificial meal with each other and gods. However, term "sacrifice" refers more to any offering into sacred fire (milk, butter, etc.) than to offering animals. Some of the Vedic rituals are continued to the present day. Sacrifice was offered to the god Soma (plant god), Agni (god of fire), and Brihaspati (god of Priestly power). Besides these gods, there was warrior Indra, the wind Vayu, storm gods or Maruts, and the sky contained the sky god Dyaus who has same origins as Zeus, Varuna who was a god of the cosmic law, Mitra who was the god of night and Vishnu.

- ## *Epic, Puranic and Classical Age (500 BCE -500 CE)*

This is the period which saw the composition of Dharma Sutras and Shastras, Mahabharata and Ramayana and Puranas which had many stories that are popular even today. The idea of Dharma is specified in Dharma Sutras and Shastras. During this period sacrifice was minimized, and the rise of the Gupta Empire (320- 500 CE) saw the evolution of the Vaishnavism, Shaivism, and Shaktism. Present-day Hinduism has many elements from this period, such as devotion and temple worship and the most important element from this period were the texts composed in Sanskrit in the form of the poetic literature.

- ## *Medieval Period (500 CE- 1500 CE)*

This period saw the rise of devotion to the main deities, especially Vishnu, Shiva and Devi. Regional kingdoms were established just after the collapse of Gupta empire, and all of them had different religions and belief systems. During this period, many of the most important temples were raised, such as Jaganatha in Puri, and two Shiva temples in Tamilnadu. The temples were dedicated to the one, major deity and were the centers of the religious and political power.

- ## *Pre-Modern Period (1500 CE -1757 CE)*

At this period, many temples were destroyed by Turkish sultanate and Hindu practices were restricted. This period is the period of poetry, meditation, yoga and Islamic mysticism. The poetry of princess Mirabai, Surdas, Dadu and many other are popular even in present day.

• *British Period (1757 CE -1947 CE)*

This period was the period of British supremacy in India. In 1757. Robert Clive won a battle at Plassey which meant the end of the Mughul Empire. Until the arrival of missionaries, British did not intend to interfere with the religion of Indian people. After the arrival of missionaries who promoted Christianity and had a strong will to westernize the local popularity, there were many Indians who converted to Christianity.

In 19 century, we can see many important reformers of the Hinduism. Reformers such as Ram Morah Roy had the intention to present the Hinduism to the world as the rational and ethical religion. All of the other reformers wanted to get rid of superstition in Hinduism. The most important person in establishing the independent India was Gandhi (1869 – 1948) who propounded non-violence, justice and love between all the people, no matter on religion. Mohandas Mahatma Gandhi is known as a "Father of India". Gandhi was assassinated in 1948.

• *Independent India (1947 CE- today)*

Indian independence resulted, in the beginning, with the nationalistic tendencies which resulted with the eruption of communal violence. Tensions were provoked by many efforts to of other religions to convert Hindus people. These tensions brought the question of Hindu identity and were the main reason for the Indians migration to Britain and U. S. A. From the 1960s until today Hindu communities all around the world became well established and socially accepted.

Hinduism recognizes single deity and other gods and goddess are just a manifestation or aspects of the Supreme God. Fundamental Hindu deities are the trinity of Brahma, Vishnu, and Shiva. Brahma is a creator, Visnu preserves, and Shiva is the one who destroys.

Gautama Buddha and Buddhism

Buddhism is another one of the world's major religions with estimated following numbers reaching over 500 million for all schools combined. The religion is most popular in East and Southeast Asia, but there are minority populations of adherents spread throughout the globe. There are two main branches of the religion, mirroring cultural differences in the region. Whence arose the world's fourth largest religion by adherents?

Buddha is technically a title, and all living things can become a Buddha through study and working towards that goal. However, Gautama Buddha is the man whose teachings are the basis for Buddhism. He lived and taught in ancient India sometime between 2600 and 2400 years ago, which makes Buddhism one of the oldest religions that are still widely practiced today. Sometimes he is referred to as The Buddha for his central role in founding the religion. Similarly to Christmas for Christians, there are celebrations in Buddhist nations to celebrate his birthday.

His early life was spent in royalty, where his father wanted him to become a king. He was shielded from the suffering of the people and how people inevitably aged; however, on a trip outside the palace, he is said to have encountered an old man. This caused him to later seek more trips, further beyond the palace grounds, and during these trips, he encountered even more suffering, including a subject suffering from disease and a corpse. These encounters resulted in him deciding to lead the life of an ascetic. Asceticism is the practice of denouncing earthly pleasures in favor of spiritual ascension. At one point he was offered the throne in another area but refused. His practices became more extreme until he had restricted himself to eating only a leaf or nut per day. Of course, this was not enough energy to sustain his body, and he collapsed while bathing one day. He was rescued and reconsidered his goals.

He knew that awakening was achieved through meditation,

but extreme asceticism to the point of starvation was not the way to achieve it. He decided on the Middle Path, which is a central tenet of Buddhism today. This is a balance between overindulgence and extreme deprivation. He is said to subsequently have meditated for 49 days under a tree until he reached True Enlightenment, which would liberate him from the cycle of rebirth, suffering, and dying that all unenlightened creatures were trapped in.

He died at the age of 80, though the records of the exact year differ based on Chinese or Sri Lankan writings. He told his disciples to follow no leader, and he believed he was entering the deathless state since he had broken out of the cycle of life and death. Relics exist of him, including some in Burma believed to be given to some of his earliest followers. His teachings were passed into the Sangha, the community of followers. They remained unsectarian for at least one hundred years after the Buddha's death when there was a documented split in the community.

The Buddha was somewhat reluctant to ordain women into the Sangha, and he even rejected his own foster mother. However, after the rejection, she felt so strongly about his teaching and awakening that she led a group of women on a long journey. After five years of further consideration and the promotion of the idea of women in the order by the Buddha's cousin, he judged that women and men both had equal rights to attain Enlightenment. Women have more rules to follow, though.

While the religion arose in India, it was eventually supplanted by Hinduism and Islam there. Nevertheless, it still holds a strong position in other parts of Asia. There two main schools of thought: Theravada and Mahayana. The former follows the Middle Way, which seeks nirvana to break the cycle of life and death, and has its strongest following in Sri Lanka and other parts of Southeast Asia. The latter sect, conversely, does not try to break out of the cycle of life and death; rather, it seeks to attain Buddhahood by staying in the cycle but teaching others how to reach awakening. This is more common in East Asia.

Dukkha is often translated as "suffering," but the English word does not quite capture the meaning. The suffering arises from being attached to transitory states, such as life and material things. One example is how vanity causes suffering because humans inevitably age. Material things also age, such as a building becoming corroded over time or even the collapse of cliffs into the ocean. Unfortunately, this attachment traps the non-enlightened in a cycle of life, death, and rebirth. To escape it, one must master the Eightfold Path, which is also known as the Middle Way. We suffer because we seek happiness from impermanent things and states (such as living), so we can never hold onto the happiness forever; hence we suffer at some point. Moreover, dukkha arises from wanting to be AWAY from such things as death. This is still a craving for something that is impermanent, and all of these cravings produce karma, which ties the creature to the cycle. Once all craving is conquered, no more karma is produced, which implies the end of rebirth. This state is known as nirvana.

Nothing in Buddhism is permanent, even the self. The notion of a linear soul, such that is common in Western religions, is untrue in Buddhism. This mistake, as described by Buddhism, is a major cause of the clinging. A person wants to be oneself and see oneself endure, through life and death and time, but that insinuates one is still clinging to something; unfortunately, that implies the production of karma and therefore no attainment of nirvana.

Those who have not reached nirvana will be reborn into one of six (or five for Theravadins) classes: heavenly, the highest, followed by ademi-god, human, animal, hungry ghost, and, at the lowest level, hellish. In the East Asian and Tibetan tradition, there is a waiting period between death and rebirth, but in the Theravadin tradition there is no such wait and immediately following death, there is arebirth. The more positive karma one has built, the higher likelihood of being reborn into a higher realm

Karma is of two types: positive and negative. The "seeds" need not mature in this life, and a deed's seed may indeed arise in the next life or even later. This reinforces the common notion surrounding karma that something having happened in a previous life has led to the current situation. Karma is not produced only by actions but also thoughts or inactions. The intention is essential to determining whether Karma is produced: the inadvertent, unknown killing of a creature does not translate into negative karmic seeds. Furthermore, karma is transferrable between family members or ancestors, and it can be accumulated not only through good deeds but by exchanging goods or services that lead to good outcomes.

Nirvana is the state of not wishing for anything, including for nirvana. This is generally considered the ultimate goal of a Buddhist, especially one who practices monastic life. However, most followers of Buddhism certainly are not monks in monasteries and for that reason, the main goal of most adherents is to increase karma for higher levels of rebirth. As the level of rebirth is elevated, it becomes more possible to lead a monastic life, or at least a life in which one becomes less interested in pursuing impermanent states. Therefore, while at first glance it may seem a bit contradictory to *want* to achieve a higher rebirth, it can also be viewed as a way to reach nirvana in the future.

The Middle Way or the Eightfold Path was the way laid out by the Buddha to follow to the cessation of dukkha, in turn becoming Enlightened. There are, obviously, 8 parts to the idea. First is the Right View and Right Resolve, which deal with wisdom. One should believe in an afterlife that is evident through life, death, and rebirth; and one should move towards loving kindness and away from cruelty. The next three, Right Speech, Right Action, and Right Livelihood, all deal with moralistic virtues. One should not lie or speak for others for the first and for the last one should not cheat or harm others with their livelihood. If possible, one should possess only the things necessary for sustenance. For Right Action, the tenets are similar to religions and codes around the world, where one should not kill or injure living creatures, one should not steal, and one should refrain from sexual misconduct. The final set of three deal with meditation, and they are Right Effort (guarding against sensual thoughts to avoid disruption to meditation), Right Mindfulness (always be conscious of one's actions), and Right Concentration (correctly meditating or concentrating).

The religion can be described as nontheistic in that there are no gods to worship as in other religions. One should respect and praise the Buddha, but that does not mean one should worship the Buddha. Furthermore, the spirits who have reached the heavenly states sometimes think of themselves as gods, but they should not require worship. Because this state has little possibility of doing ill deeds and gaining negative karma, sometimes the spirits there remain for very long periods of time. Due to the long lengths of time spent in such sublime planes of existence, a spirit there can be deluded into thinking it is a god. However, there is no required worship in Buddhism.

Aztec, Mayan, and Incan Religions

The Mayan religion was a polytheistic one that had a hierarchy with a Supreme God. This god was too sacred to partake in daily human affairs, and as such was not present in the ways people went about their lives. His son was the god of books and writing and the champion of science. This gives an indication of how important science and learning was for the Mayans. Similarly to many polytheistic mythologies, there are a plethora of gods who have various aspects associated with them. These aspects are connected to real world phenomena or concepts in human societies (such as science and learning).

As is common even with modern South American tribal beliefs, the Mayans believed the world had been destroyed and recreated many times. The cosmology surrounding the earth was complex, with 9 levels of the underworld and 13 levels of heaven. The same gods ruled over all these planes. And showing similarity with other magic-based religions, each god had a specific color (often colors are associated with gods and emotions because certain colors evoke certain emotions more strongly than others). The idea of levels was also present in the monuments built by Mayans, presented in the form of pyramids. The pyramids generally had a temple on the top, but the pyramid itself was a set of steps to the gods. Often when the ruler died, his successor would build another pyramid on top of the one already there.

The priesthood was not celibate, in deep contrast to the Catholic Spanish and Portuguese who came later. That is important, too, because initiation into the priesthood was hereditary, and if there were no reproduction by the priests, the priesthood would quickly die out. Sacrifice was common, mostly of various animals. However, human sacrifice was considered the holiest and human blood was the essence on which the gods thrived. Usually, slaves, criminals, and orphans were the offerings for such sacrifices. Another violent aspect of Mayan traditional beliefs was to start bloodletting after the beginning of ceremonies by piercing various parts of the face and head.

Like the Mayans (and indeed the common theme among South American Natives), the Aztecs believed in the destruction and rebirth of the world. The world had died four times, and our current world is the fifth reincarnation. They believed the two sources of everything were two beings, and they lived in the 13th level of heaven (the levels reflect the Mayans' beliefs). This highest level of heaven was considered the be a very cold place, and may have its very ancient origin in the fact that the northern and southern latitude of the world are rather cold places.

The cold place was where man originated (interestingly, it is thought by modern historians that people migrated to the Americas over a land bridge between Russia and Alaska, so this may actually be a legend that has truth behind it). All the gods were created by the two top gods, and the birth of the sun, which was essential to life, was only possible through blood and sacrifice. This violent belief led many sacrifices, though the acts were not due to Aztec cruelty, as some Westerns believe. The sacrifice was a way to keep the world alive, and the duty of the sacrificed was to bear a message to the gods to let the sun be born again. The sun god was the central figurehead in the hierarchy of the Aztecs (the two origin beings created all the gods), and as the Aztecs conquered more land, his importance rose.

The Aztecs were interested in absorbing other religions and beliefs, and they did not necessarily have to conflict with Aztec beliefs. This is a common theme for empires, which will assimilate the beliefs of the conquered into their societies, thereby quelling unrest in newly subjugated populations.

Further south, the Inca had differently named gods but their roles often ran alongside those of the other civilizations. There was a central creator god who made nature, while there was also a sun god among others. The Inti Raymi festival was their largest celebration and celebrates the winter solstice. Various indigenous cultures in the Andes Mountains still celebrate today, though many have equated the celebrations with the Christian holiday of St. John the Baptist.

Huacas are Incan spiritual places, and these could be placed in caves, near springs, or in man-made shrines. The battlefields and cemeteries are also appropriate places for the spiritual worship of the gods. On the concept of sacrifice, it was mostly animal sacrifice and human sacrifice was rare. However, if it was deemed that the animal sacrifices were not providing sufficient results, a human sacrifice was prescribed. Different animals were sacrificed to specific gods.

Of course, the rulers of all the empires used religion for their own ends, too. Throughout history, in Native American and in other societies, rulers have used religious arguments to take their place at the seat of power. If it seems like a backward idea, consider that even the French kings not long ago used the divine right to continue their rule. Just the same, the Aztec, Incan, and Mayan rulers used religion as a way to enforce their power and protect their seat at the throne.

Native American Religions

When most Westerners think of Native American religions, there are images of totem poles, ritual dances, Aztec sacrifices, and spiritual drug use. These are all part of Native American religions, but the scope goes far beyond just those four ideas. Certainly, vastly diverse cultures spread out over two continents and millennia are not so standardized as to be conceptualized in just four notions. The style of religion ranges over all types, from mono- and polytheistic to animistic and henotheistic, which focuses on a single god but acknowledges the possibility of other deities.

The religions were largely disseminated through oral traditions. This meant over generations the religion could evolve rapidly and change significantly. The keepers of the traditions were medicine men and shamans, who were able to communicate with the gods. These positions were highly esteemed and elevated the holder's position in society, such that they were given responsibilities for major decisions and ceremonies. However, as a result of this lack of written accounts, many European invaders, and even many modern people, did not see the religions as true religions, for they are not prescriptive in nature and do not have historical, written accounts. And perhaps they are correct, for Native American religions are actually more spiritual beliefs that do not separate worlds.

Aside from the population decimation faced by the indigenous of the Americas, their religion was under attack by Europeans who sent missionaries to convert the natives to Christianity. The mixture of death brought on by war and disease plus the conversion efforts has effectively obliterated the religions, though there are still some elements that survive in the tight-knit communities of Natives. After the formation of the United States, the federal government combatted the native religions by forcibly removing children from their families and placing them into western style schools. This continued well into the modern age, with the practice still being practiced as late as the 1970s. This has left the population of those practicing Native American religions to be tiny, with only about 9000 estimated to be in the United States today. However, that number is deemed an underestimate since being a member of the society is not required to practice the religion.

As is common with ancient religions, the beliefs held were largely used to explain physical phenomena that occurred in nature. This led to many animals being representative of different aspects of nature, for what better embodies nature than a living creature within it? The idea that nature and everything physical can be connected runs deep in such traditions. There is little if any boundary between this world and others if other worlds are believed to exist. However, the beliefs are highly localized, and it is impossible to expound on all the variations in this short book.

One major theme that is common throughout the highly varied belief systems is location. Location is often directly embedded into the system such that nearby mountains or rivers can hold significance for one group. Therefore, by the very nature of the religious system, it becomes localized and necessarily different from others. Other common themes are that words and knowledge have power; sometimes so much power that special ritualistic preparation is required to wield such knowledge. Participating in the community is also more important than belief, which strongly promotes a collective mindset over an individual one. This intertwining of participation and religion means acting in the best interests of the community and helping others in it are considered religious as well as social acts.

Due to the loss of so many tribes and so much knowledge during the European invasion, a lot of native religions have simply disappeared. There are some rays of hope, though, for the Native American Church, and the Ghost Dance movements have both revived interested in traditional ways. It originated in the mid-19th century and, ironically, spread through the Indian schools set up by the US government to combat traditional beliefs – the pupils were able to communicate with each other over distances which facilitated the spread. It blends traditional practices and Christianity in a religion that is not tied to location. Today it is practiced throughout the country (albeit on a very small scale). The Ghost Dance was a backlash against the ever-expanding greed of the American and European settlers. The movement was a way to promote the revival of native religion after decimation and constant erosion from European forces. The movement suffered a major blow when the natives lost at Wounded Knee at the end of the 19th century, though it still saw some implementation until the 1950s and a few revivals later.

As the traditions were largely oral, it is believed by many practitioners that the rituals only have importance in the original language. Unfortunately, this does not bode well for the religions, as the languages of the natives are rapidly dying out in a constantly standardizing world. Furthermore, if there is no way to translate the concept into English (or any other language for that matter), it is far too easy for the knowledge to simply disappear altogether. Furthermore, if the place is important, so can artifacts be important. Unfortunately, again, many of these have been taken to museums where their power to the people who worship or use them is absolutely diminished. One reason single objects can be so powerful for these practices is that, as mentioned, everything is alive and flowing with some sort of energy. This includes seemingly inanimate objects such as masks and dress.

On the other hand, in South America, the communities that still practice indigenous religions are alive and well. Most have been influenced at least to a degree by Christianity, but it is certainly not the only option open to adherents. Sometimes these religions even incorporate Christian beliefs, pitting a Christ-like savior hero against the invading colonists and imperial destruction of their lands.

The movement of stars and the passage of time are central to many of these belief systems, and this idea is even evident in the Western obsession with the Mayan calendar. Many South

American systems also include some sort of destruction of many worlds, which incites an interesting question of why powerful figures and world fall to disarray. It is believed the idea of the destruction of worlds predates the invasion of Europeans, but the absolute destruction of many tribal ways of life surely attributed some truth to these beliefs.

The spiritual journey undertaken by many shamans are for the purpose of communicating with the other worlds or for finding religious answers. Strong herbal mixtures were common in inducing altered states of mind, which assisted the traveler in his quest. Two common substances were Mescal and peyote cactus, both of which are sometimes used recreationally by non-natives to alter their mind states. For shamans, the spirit is able to exit the body once a trance state is achieved and can wander. The shaman takes greatly detailed note of the surroundings and is eventually expected to find a path forward in life. Animal and plant spirits may show themselves to the quester during the journey for further guidance. The shaman must then return to his body and should have solutions for the tribe.

History of Religion in America (From Native Americans to Present-day)

With the arrival of missionaries, Native Americans were the object of many extensive Christian activities.

Protestant faith motivated the first European settlers to establish their community from Europe to the New World where they could practice their religion in peace. Ever since then, America became a synonym for freedom of religion and religious refugee for all the Europeans who were faced with religious persecution and who refused to compromise and accept conservative Christian religious doctrines in Europe. Europeans wanted to escape from the Roman Catholic Church and the Church of England whose religious beliefs they found too oppressive and forced. America was supposed to be a new world where the state and church would be separated, and everyone would have a right to practice their religion without being afraid of persecution.

From the colonial times to the present-day, evangelism has played the essential role in the history of religion in America. The most important Christian denominations in America were:

- ***Puritans***

Reformed Presbyterian churches, as well as the European Free Church, gave a base to the reforms which were brought in America by Puritans. Puritans were English Protestants tended to „purify „ the Church of England resulting in the birth of first Baptists and Congregationalists in America. Around 900 puritans, together with their leader John Winthrop, and books that were printed to spread the „Good News „ settled down in Massachusetts Bay. Their tradition of taking care of each other turned this number of 900 to grow to more than

100,000 until 1700. Puritans based their life on the teaching of John Calvin and the New Testament. Puritans were considered to be a group of extremists who believed that traditional, deep-rooted church must not be reformed and that only solution was to separate the churches. Puritans believed that an individual, as well as the group, exist only to glory and honor the God and that their primary task in this life is to the God`s will. They hold on to the belief that their destiny was predetermined and their segregation, isolation, and religious singularity later lead to the witch hunts starting in 1688.

• *Congregationalists*

Congregationalism is more easily classified as a movement. The early Congregationalists believed in the idea of pure church. Congregationalists planted their beliefs and traditions based on Calvinists (Reformed) established practice, strictly disputing the external authorities. Congregationalists came to New England in 1620 and created the autonomous congregations in which God was the unconditional authority. Most important Congregationalists that formed divided churches from the Church of England were Robert Brown, Henry Barrow, John Greenwood, John Penry, Thomas Jollie, and John Robinson. Some of the first colleges and universities in America, such as Harvard, Yale, and Middlebury, etc. were founded by Congregationalists.

• *Methodists*

The base of the Methodism was a group of students from the Oxford University. Unlike Puritans, Methodists were not departing from Europe because of the religious persecution. They developed their religious inspiration from the teachings of John Wesley. Besides John Wesley, important leaders of this movement were George Whitefield and brother of John Wesley- Charles Wesley. Theology of Methodists was concentrated on dedication and effect of faith on human's nature. Methodist beliefs accentuate the promise of salvation, justness, and righteousness, as well as the perfection of love, support for the sick and charity. Methodists established hospitals, orphanages, soup kitchens, and schools. Methodists rejected the Calvinists beliefs that God has predetermined salvation of chosen group of people.

• *Lutherans*

Lutheranism is a leading and most prominent branch of Protestant Christianity and
Lutheran Church played the most important role in the history of American Christian denomination. Members of the Lutheran Church came from all sides of Europe: Germany, Sweden, Denmark, Finland, and Norway. Lutheranism promotes an attitude of justification "by grace alone through faith alone on the basis of Scripture alone." It is established on the belief that humanity possesses free will on "goods and possessions" but that it is also sinful by nature and helpless or impotent when it comes to contributing to its own salvation. Lutherans find the Jesus is the Christ, promised savior and both by nature man and God. They came to America in 1619 and settled on the East Coast and American Midwest. From their first foothold, they established 150 synods.

• *Presbyterians*

Presbyterian and Reformed churches share the same prevalent root in the teachings of John Calvin and the Swiss Reformation. Having a little in common with the liturgy and tradition correlated with a Roman Catholic Church, Presbyterian denomination is more attached to an active leadership style for ministers and lay members. They came to America from England, Scotland and Ireland with named Presbyterians that worked with the congregation's ordained minister. Presbyterian's belief structures and practices are bringing to the focus the Bible and the sovereignty of God. Nowadays, they make up one of the most extensive branches of Protestant Christianity.

• *Quakers*

Quakers were established by English evangelist George Fox, in 1647. Quakers belief system was based on the idea that one's conscience is the furthermost important authority on morals and actions. One of the most important members of Quakers was William Penn. He wrote about freedom of consciousness, and his writings made a base of religious ideas and understandings for Quakers all around the world. William Penn wrote about and believed in equal rights for women and promoted religious toleration. He also accentuated the need for fair trade with Native Americans. Quakers did not have church buildings and they spoke up only when "the Spirit moved them." Being very modest, Quakers dressed up in plain clothes and preferred simple life over aristocracy.

The most important Christian churches that had a great influence on the history of religion in America were Roman Catholicism, Anglicanism, and Eastern Orthodoxy.

These, often called "liturgical" churches set form of ritualistic practices and practiced an allegiance to certain doctrines that were based in the early centuries.

Even though not the oldest one, Roman Catholic Church ranks as the largest Christian tradition today. Roman Catholics arrived in America with Spanish people in 1513. In the beginning, Roman Catholics held their cultural roots strongly, however, later they joining the rest of the American society. Even though there are many members of Roman Catholic Church that do not agree with all the issues, such as abortion, the general attitude towards woman and abortion, the American Church has continued its loyalty to the Pope even today.

The Church of England, which later became the Episcopal Church in the U. S. was the first one established in America, in Virginia. Ever since their first services were held, The Church of England had been tested by a numerous schism, especially when it comes to their attitude toward woman. The Church of England and Roman Church are in many ways similar, especially in their clergy orders.

Orthodoxy is the third Christian church which had a great influence on Christianity in America today. Eastern Orthodoxy in America is a mixture of many church bodies whose origin comes from Greece, Romania, and Russia. The Orthodox belief system is based on doctrines of the early Christianity and the Bible. Their services are the most detailed worship services of all the Christian traditions.

America was also the perfect place for utopian communities which rose as the places where followers could be involved in perfect social and religious systems. The first utopian community in America was established in 1663 and, until the American Revolution, there were about 20 of them. Throughout the history, the most successful utopian community was the Mormons community. The leader of Mormons was Joseph Smith who established these communities in Ohio, Missouri, and Illinois. Joseph Smith claimed that angled directed him to a buried book which was written on golden plates. According to Smith, this book, which he named as the Book of Mormon, contained the religious history of people. In 1830 Smith established a church of Christ, and its missionaries had made a large number of people who converted to Mormons religion. Over time, Mormons expanded their missionary efforts around Europe and South Pacific and many of the people that converted came from England and Scandinavia. Mormons believe in a universe which is ruled by a God whose goal is to bring his followers / children, immortality and eternal life. They believe in the pre-mortal existence, and that people are, at this stage, spirit children of God who created the plan of salvation which will help his children to make progress and become like him. The most important child of God is Jesus Christ, who is considered to be the eldest child and only those who fully accept the Jesus will be accepted to the highest kingdom. Mormons believe that God chose Joseph Smith to restore the Christianity the way it should be from the beginning. The popularity of utopian community escalated during the 1960s and 1970s. Many of those who were seeking for personal growth joined these communities. Utopian communities offered an alternative lifestyle which served as an example of some of the best characteristics that America was originally meant to offer.

Although Jews were presented in America in the 17th century, large-scale immigration took place only in 19th century, as a result of European persecutions. In the history of American religion, it is also very important to mention that Israel gained the statehood after the centuries of persecution and mistreatment. President Harry S. Truman offered U. S. A. `s recognition if the Israel statehood for the sake of all those who suffered in the World War 2. Even though there was a possibility of retaliation from Arab countries, President Harry S. Truman also offered recognition of the American Jewish population and, no matter on the long criticism America continued to support Israel notably among American evangelical churches. From 1950s African- American Southern churches also created a sustained presence on the American religious scene as a result of impassioned leaders such as Martin Luther King and Malcolm X. New Age movement in America emerged in 1968. New Agers started looking for the answers in spirituality and occult, identifying themselves with the wave of the Eastern spiritual masters. The idea of the New Age movement was bonding with the God on the basis of universal transformation. The fastest spreading and developing manifestation of the movement is Scientology founded by L. Ron Hubbard in 1954. Scientology is based on Hubbard` s researches and analysis of how the human mind and spirit work.

Nowadays, America continues to be a place for all of those who seek for religious freedom and, with approximately 3,000 religious groups that exist on its territory makes a small heaven for every human being.

Abrahamic Religions

Abrahamic religions are one of the major religions in the world. Judaism, Christianity, and Islam are the largest divisions in comparative religion in terms of numbers of followers. Of all these three Abrahamic religions, Judaism, Christianity, and Islam, Judaism is the oldest Abrahamic religion, and it dates from the late second millennium BCE.

Christianity first occurred in the first century BCE, while the Islam is the youngest among these three and dates from seventh century BCE. Besides these three main religions, there are also Samaritanism, the Duze faith, Rastafari, and Baha I Faith which are also Abrahamic religions.

Term "Abrahamic religion" means that these religions come from one metaphysical origin- belief in Abraham as the ancestor. While Christians assign Abraham as a "father in faith," Muslims have a religious term "faith of Ibrahim" which illustrates the belief that practicing the Islam is based on traditions of Abraham. All three Abrahamic religions claim their genealogies to Abraham in their sacred texts. In Torah, Abraham is described as the ancestor of the Israelites, the first part of Christian Bible- Old Testament, also claim Abraham as their ancestor, and Islamic tradition claims that Muhammad is a descended of Ishmael who is a descendant of Isaac by Jacob, who is later known as Israel. There are many common elements to Judaism, Christianity, and Islam:

- ## *Monotheism*

Christianity, Judaism, and Islam are strictly monotheistic religions which promote the faith in one omnipotent and omnipresent God, creator of the entire universe. As an opposite of the ancient polytheistic religions such as Mesopotamian and Egyptian, followers of the Abrahamic religions are not created only to serve the gods. Abrahamic system of belief is based on faith in one God who cared about his creation (people) and desires the well-being of all human beings. For the safety of human kind, it is believed that God has provided basic rules which, if followed, make a man good and righteous. In Jewish theology, God of Israel is the God of Abraham, Isaac, and Jacob. The God of Israelites is named YHWH (Jehovah) which means "The self-existent One." Although Christians believe in holy trinity the Father, the Son, and the Holy Spirit, it is still monotheistic religion, and the belief in the Trinity is just an expression of the complex divinity of the God. Islamic belief, on the opposite of Christianity, has no progeny. Islamic God is named Allah.

• *Religious texts*

It is believed that religious texts were God's tool of communicating with people. This way God was able to express his will to the human kind. Even though all the main Abrahamic religions have their own sacred texts, those texts feature very similar figures, historical stories / myths, and places. These religious texts are considered to be words of God, therefore sacred and unquestionable. The sacred scriptures of Judaism are Torah (Law of Teachings), Nevi`im (Prophets) and Ketuwim (Writings). Most of the Christian groups take the Old Testament and the New Testament for their sacred scriptures. Latin Bible contained 73 books, but 7 of them were removed by Martin Luther King because of the lack of original Hebrew sources. Islam`s holiest book is the Qur'an. However, Muslims do believe in the religious texts of Judaism and Christianity as well, but only in their original versions which, they believed, are lost by many years of changing and rewriting.

• *Good and Evil*

Judaism, Christianity, and Islam strongly believe in the choice between good and evil. Abrahamic religions have actually the came concept and ethical orientation which is associated with the obedience or disobedience to a God.

[61]

• *Judgment day*

All the Abrahamic religions are based on the belief in Judgment day. Beginning with the creation of the world, through the entire history of humanity, all the way to the death and the day of final Judgment when it is believed, true followers will go to heaven, and those who disobeyed will go to hell. Even described differently, all the religions spread the story of heaven and hell. What is the most fascinating is that, on the opposite of traditional belief, none of these religions claim that followers of the other religion will strictly go to hell. The most important goal in anyone`s life, no matter on religion, is to follow main moral instructions and do no harm to any other living creature on purpose.

• *Prophets*

Abrahamic religions had prophets who were, besides the sacred texts, a God`s tool to communicate with people. Abraham is claimed to be the first Hebrew and father of Jewish people, Jesus Christ was a prophet of Christianity, the son of the God, and Muslims believe in Muhammad a.s. As mentioned, all three of these religions do believe that Abraham was their ancestor, and Muslims actually believe in all the Abrahamic prophets, considering the Muhammad as the last one whose primary goal was to bring back the basics of monotheistic religion.

• *Rituals and Traditions*

Abrahamic religions have some very similar rituals and traditions, starting from the fact that all of them have one day in a week to rest and do nothing. This is considered to be based on the story of how God created the world in six days, and the last one took to take a rest. In Judaism it is Sabbath, Christians have Sundays and Muslim people Friday.

Nowadays, since Abrahamic religions take the majority of the world's religions, we can see many tensions between the followers of these three religions. No matter on some disagreements it is the fact that these religions have many things in common and while the extremists are taking the effort to find the differences, regular people, no matter which Abrahamic religion they follow, learned from their religion that they should not hate any God`s creature.

History of Jerusalem

The Israeli city of Jerusalem has a complex and bloody 6,000-year story. At the beginning of its history, a group of people made a settlement near the Gihon Spring, which lies east of today's Old City walls. For hundreds of years, Jerusalem was merely a small place dominated by agricultural concerns. It was known as Rusalimum, and may have referred to Shalim, a Canaanite dawn god. At the time, the Egyptian empire was powerful, and the inhabitants of the settlement would have lived under its rule.

Two and a half thousand years after it was founded, Jerusalem and the surrounding area were invaded by a group of people known as the Philistines. They weakened the Egyptian empire's rule. King David emerged as a ruler, creating a new kingdom (Judea), which had Jerusalem as its capital. The city became subject to the increasingly organized rule. The inhabitants officially worshiped a single god, but ancient polytheistic beliefs were still the day-to-day norm. A Temple was built, and the population was encouraged to make religious pilgrimages there and cast their old religions aside.

Ahaz of Jerusalem was king of Judea in 733 BCE. At that time, he requested that the ruler of the Assyrian Empire help him defeat his enemy and neighbor, Israel. However, the Babylonians defeated the Assyrians in 605 BCE. Their king, Nebuchadnezzar, later took over Jerusalem and took the king of Jerusalem, Jehoiachin, into captivity. Zedekiah was made king in his place but was still subject to control by Nebuchadnezzar. However, he rebelled in 587 BCE and as a result, the latter destroyed the Temple in a fit of rage. After a period of conflict, Jerusalem was left empty for a number of years.

When the Babylonian empire collapsed in 538 BCE, the new ruler King Cyrus II of Persia encouraged an alliance with the Judeans by allowing them to rebuild their Temple. By 516

BCE, the new Temple was complete, and Jerusalem became the administrative center of Judea, now ruled over by the Persians. A comprehensive history is beyond the scope of this chapter but, in brief, Jerusalem was ruled by the following groups and leaders: Alexander The Great, Ptolemy I, the Seleucid Empire, the Hasmoneans (including King Herod, who was installed by the Roman Empire), Nero, Titus, Emperor Hadrian, Umar ibn al-Khattab, the Umayyad dynasty, the Fatimid dynasty, the Crusaders, the Mamluks, and the Ottoman Empire, who ruled for almost 400 years. During the Ottoman rule, which was largely tolerant and peaceful, the city expanded to include a number of new settlements beyond its official walls.

Jerusalem has been completely ruined on two occasions, subjected to over 20 sieges, over 40 instances of capture and recapture, and 52 instances of attack. For significant periods in Jerusalem's history, Jews were banned from living in or sometimes even visiting the city. In 312 CE, Christian rule exiled Jews from the city. Jews were permitted to live there once more in 638 CE whilst the city was under Muslim rule, but mosques were built on Temple Mount, previously a holy Jewish site of special religious significance. In 1099, the city's Muslim rulers were defeated by Christians and the city's Jews were killed. It wasn't until 1267 that a new synagogue was established.

The British ruled Jerusalem from 1917-1948, after which it was split into two parts – one-half belonged to Jordan, and the other to Israel. Israel took control of Jerusalem in 1967 during the Six-Day War against Egypt, Syria, and Jordan. Modern-day Jerusalem is split between Jews in the west and Muslims and Christians in the east.

History of the Church

To speak of the history of 'the Church' is to speak of the history of Christianity, which encompasses various branches of the religion and its attendant figures, buildings, and nations. Early Church history began with the early spread of Christianity in the middle of the first century AD. The early Christians took their religion from Jerusalem and brought it to Jordan and Egypt. By the end of the third century AD, Christianity was a major religious force in the Mediterranean.

The missionary Paul (formerly known as Saul prior to his conversion) played a major role in spreading Christianity. He worked hard in establishing groups of Christians – churches – in many countries, both within and beyond the Roman Empire. However, despite his efforts, Christians were often persecuted for their beliefs by various rulers including Nero (54-68) and Diocletian (284-305). As a result, Christians were often martyrs, dying in an attempt to uphold their faith.

A key change took place when a senior Roman soldier, Constantine, triumphed in an important battle in his quest to become Emperor. He believed that the Christian God had helped him succeed, and as a result converted to the religion. Shortly afterward, Christianity became the approved, official religion of the Roman Empire and Christians could live without fear of persecution. In order to formulate the specifics of the Christian religion, Constantine called a council together in Nicea in 325 AD. They established creeds and the official tenets of the Christian faith.

However, their decisions did not go unchallenged. Over the coming centuries, various figures would launch counter-attacks and alternative interpretations of, for example, the teachings of Jesus. The final Council held to discuss such matters during the time of the Roman Empire was held in 451 AD in Chalcedon. The Roman Empire fell in 476 AD, and the impact upon the Christian Church was significant. Previously, all members of the Church had been subject to Roman rule.

However, once the Empire collapsed, differences between Eastern and Western Christians emerged.

Various differences in opinion regarding teachings and traditions within the Church erupted into the Great Schism in 1054. The religious rulers of Constantinople and Rome were unable to reconcile their views, and the Church was split into two main branches – the Orthodox and Roman Catholic Churches. A key difference concerns the issue of Papal infallibility. The Roman Catholic Church recognizes the authority of the Pope, whereas the Orthodox Church does not.

Between the 14th and 15th century, there was a significant difference of opinion within the Roman Catholic Church concerning the appointment of a new Pope. This resulted in a fresh schism, which was motivated by political as much as religious issues. Another key turning point in Church history was the Protestant Reformation, which began in 1517 when a German monk by the name of Martin Luther began to protest against what he saw as problematic issues within the Church, such as the buying of indulgences and general corruption. In time, a number of groups would form including the Lutherans, the Calvinists, the Reformed, and Anabaptist churches. Small groups who were considered to have 'radical beliefs' (such as the Amish and the Hutterites) were persecuted by the larger, more well-established branches of the Church. Later movements within the Church included Puritanism (16th and 17th Centuries), Pietism, and Spiritual Revivalism (incorporating the 18th Century Methodist movement, which represented a breakaway group from the Church of England).

Today there are over two billion Christians around the world. There are three key denominational branches, 12 denominational families, and 33,000 denominational sects. The Catholic, Eastern Orthodox, and Oriental Orthodox Churches all claim to be the one true Church grounded in the teachings of Jesus, meaning that Christianity remains a highly divided religion.

Crusades

'The Crusades' is a phrase that generally refers to several long-term military operations led by the Church that took place during the Medieval period (between the 11th and 15th centuries) with the intention of defeating Muslims living in the Middle East. It is important to note that there is no universal agreement among historians as to how exactly, a 'crusade' ought to be defined. However, the information in this section is generally considered representative of the history and purpose of the Crusades. The purpose of the Crusades was to secure Christian territory, to capture lands held by those of other faiths, and to defend Christians living under the threat of persecution in other lands.

The campaign referred to as the First Crusade was triggered in 1095 following Pope Urban II's statement that the Byzantine Empire needed the Church's help in defeating Turks in Anatolia. Pope Urban claimed that he wanted to ensure rights of access to areas in the Holy Land that were under Muslim rule, but his actual motives remain unclear. He may have sought, rather, to bring together Western and Eastern regions of Christendom before establishing himself as head of a new Church.

Those who lead Crusades would often use their positions to further their own ends, sometimes keeping the lands they captured for themselves rather than aim to establish a new, peaceful Christian kingdom. For example, those leading armed units in the First Crusade did not always return the land to the Byzantines.

Those leading the First Crusade achieved their goal of capturing Jerusalem in 1099 and established Christian states in the surrounding areas. Centuries of fraught relationships between various groups in the region lead to further Crusades, all of which were ordered by Papal authority with variously stated intentions. For example, the Fifth Crusade featured the invasion of Egypt, and the Sixth Crusade the restoration of the holy city of Jerusalem. The final Crusade, lead by King St. Louis IX of France in 1269, represented an invasion of Tunisia. In brief, the eight Crusades were as follows:

The First Crusade: 1096-1099: Jerusalem was recaptured from Muslim rulers in 1099.

The Second Crusade: 1147-1149: Louis VII of France and Conrad III of Germany lead a campaign to capture the County of Edessa.

The Third Crusade: 1189-1192: Lead by three European kings with the aim of recapturing Jerusalem, which was again under Muslim rule.

The Fourth Crusade: 1202-1204: This represented another attempt at regaining the Holy City. However, it ended with the sacking of Constantinople.

The Fifth Crusade:1217-1221: An attempt to succeed where the Fourth Crusade had failed, this campaign also ended in defeat.

The Sixth Crusade: 1228-1229: A major success, this Crusade ended with the capture of Jerusalem, Nazareth, and other cities.

The Seventh Crusade: 1248-1254: Louis IX attempted to conquer Egypt and recapture parts of the Holy Land that had fallen outside of Christian rule. However, he failed as he had to return home to France when his mother died.

The Eighth Crusade: 1270: This represented Louis' second attempt. He began in Tunisia but died shortly after arriving. His brother was left to ensure the army returned home to France. Prince Edward of England then launched his own campaign but left to return home once he received news that his father had fallen ill.

Each Crusade had the following elements in common. Firstly, all those taking part swore an allegiance to join the cause. They would sew a red cross onto their clothes, which could only be removed when they had completed their quest. Secondly, all Crusades were ordered or endorsed by the current Pope. Thirdly, those who completed their Crusade were granted leniency for their sins, also known as 'indulgences.' Finally, in order to 'count' as a Crusade, those fighting it had to be granted privileges. For instance, anyone caught attempting to take over a Crusader's lands was punished severely. Crusaders also enjoyed hospitality from the Church, and lower rates of taxes compared with those paid by the general public.

The legacy left by the Crusades is extensive. In practical terms, they facilitated business and travel in the Mediterranean area, which, in turn, meant that cities such as Venice grew in wealth and influence. The ideals of chivalry, self-denial and heroism were widely endorsed, and this lay the foundations for various literary traditions including romanticism.

Muhammad

Muhammad (Muḥammad ibn ʿAbd Allāh), also known as 'The Prophet Muhammad,' is the most important human figure within Islam. Muslims believe him to be the final prophet sent from God to humankind in order that the one true monotheistic religion is established. He is commonly referred to as 'The Holy Prophet' by followers of Islam. 'Muhammad' translates to 'praiseworthy' in Arabic. Muslims believe that Muhammad's origins can be traced back to the prophet Abraham, placing Muhammad firmly amongst the most significant prophets to have ever lived and contributed to the modern monotheistic religions.

Muhammad was born in Mecca, Arabia, circa 570 CE. His parents died young, leaving him an orphan who was raised by various relatives and non-relatives including a grandfather and then an uncle. It is thought that the Islamic tradition of showing generosity towards orphans is the direct result of the Prophet's own beginnings in life. In line with customs of the time, the young Muhammad passed a few years in the desert with the Bedouin people, in order that he might learn not only the Arabic language and traditions but also desirable personal qualities such as self-discipline.

As an adult, Muhammad worked as a merchant trader. Islamic tradition teaches that he was a good-looking man who enjoyed a reputation as a fair, noble individual who was always willing to help others. He became known as 'al-Amin,' which translates to 'The Trusted One.' Between his shoulder blades was a mole, which was recognized by many as a sign of prophet hood. At the age of 25, Muhammad married a 40-year-old widow by the name of Khadijah. Their union was long and happy. Despite the fact that it was common practice to take multiple wives, he did not marry another woman until Khadijah had died. The couple had six children, two boys (who died young) and four girls.

In middle age, he began to receive holy revelations whilst engaging in prayer and periods of quiet seclusion in caves near his home. Within a few years, he began spreading these teachings. Among Muhammad's key messages were the following: That there is only one God, that all must surrender to God, and that he (Muhammad) was a prophet in direct communication with God. He stated that he had received direct teachings from the Angel Gabriel and other holy figures.

When he received the first set of revelations from the Angel Gabriel, Muhammad feared that he had been possessed by demonic forces. He told his wife what had occurred, and she consulted her Christian cousin Waraqah. Waraqah, who was highly knowledgeable on the topic of religious and spiritual matters, believed that Muhammad had been chosen as a prophet. He would then receive revelations, which were sometimes accompanied by a bell-like sound, for 23 more years.

Initially, when Muhammad tried to tell others what he had learned, his preaching was met with hostility. He left Mecca and settled in Medina. This move came to be known as the Hijra. Whilst living in Medina, Muhammad formed a united state of tribes, known as the Constitution of Medina. In 629 CE, he and thousands of converts to Islam captured Mecca. By the time of Muhammad's death a few years later, much of the Arab world had converted to Islam.

The teachings received by Muhammad from middle age until death form the basis of the Quran, the holy text at the heart of the Islamic faith. The Quran, also known as 'The Word of God,' is comprised of verses addressing a range of issues covering most aspects of human nature and relationships. There are also separate pieces of literature – the Hadith and sira literature – that contain other teachings and practices espoused by Muhammad (also known as 'sunnah').

The World's Religions

It is commonly agreed that there are six major religions practiced around the world today. They are listed below, along with their key beliefs.

Christianity: Based on the life and teachings of Jesus Christ, a Jew who lived approximately 2,000 years ago, Christianity has 2.1 billion followers. Christians believe that Jesus was the Messiah promised in the Jewish Old Testament, that he is the son of God, and was sent to earth in order that humanity be saved from its sins. Jesus is believed to have come to earth in human form and died on the cross before rising from the dead and ascending to Heaven. Followers believe that in coming to accept Jesus as one's personal savior, one can enjoy eternal life and closeness to God. The Bible is the key holy text within Christianity.

Islam: With 1.3 billion followers, Islam is the most popular religion on Earth. The faith was formed in Arabia by the Prophet Muhammad. Islam is a monotheistic religion – indeed, the word 'Islam' means 'submission to God's will.' Muslims believe that the key teachings of Allah (God) were revealed to the Prophet Muhammad around 1500 years ago. Jesus, Abraham, and Moses are respected as prophets, but Muslims believe that the word of God was revealed in its final form to Muhammad. The Quran is the Islamic holy text.

Hinduism: Hinduism is practiced by 900 million people worldwide, and is more properly described as a group of religions and practices originating over thousands of years ago. It is unusual in that it has no key figurehead or even consensus as regards teachings. The word 'Hindu' derives from 'Sindhu,' a Sanskrit word used by inhabitants of a region of northwest India. Although it is difficult to define 'a Hindu,' most practitioners follow a body of literature called the Veda, and a system of morals known as dharma. Most Hindus believe in a supreme God who may take on a variety of forms, as well as the principle of reincarnation.

Buddhism: Derived from the teachings of the Buddha, Buddhism is practiced by 376 to over 500 million people worldwide. It focuses on attaining enlightenment through regular, deep contemplation on the true nature and meaning of existence. In the 6th century BCE, a prince by the name of Siddhartha Gautama left his life of luxury and went on a quest for personal enlightenment. Sitting underneath a tree one day, he found what he was seeking – a sense of being at one with the universe. Buddhists do not believe in a personal God and see change as the single ongoing reality. Morality, wisdom, and meditation are perceived as paths to nirvana (a state of ultimate enlightenment and bliss).

Sikhism: Practiced by 23 million people worldwide, Sikhism is based on the teachings of the teachings of Guru Nanak, who lived during the 15th Century CE. It is a monotheistic religion that has at its center an emphasis on living well and performing good deeds, not merely enacting religious rituals. A Sikh will strive to remember God at all times, serve other people, work hard, act fairly, and be honest. Sikhs worship at temples known as Gurdwaras and their religious text is the Guru Granth Sahib.

Judaism: Predating Christianity and Islam, Judaism is the religion of 14 million people across the globe. Jews believe that they were chosen over 3500 years ago to enter into an agreement with God. Under the terms of this agreement, they agreed to uphold a standard of holiness and good behavior to all other groups of people. The religion was founded by Moses. Their holy text is the Torah, which outlines the moral law. A Jewish place of worship is known as a synagogue, and their religious leaders are known as Rabbis.

The World`s Most Destructive Religious Movements / Cults

Ever since the ancient times, the world has created a great amount of religions whose primary goal was to help the person to identify himself with a group of like-minded. However, one thing which should be the same for every religion is not to do harm to any other creature. Unfortunately, today, there are many destructive groups that name themselves as some sort of religious movements whose ritual practices and system of beliefs include human sacrifice, child abuse, mass suicides, criminal activity or psychological causalities which can expose an unethical use of control. Some of the most common features of these movements are isolation, group pressure, removing any chance of privacy- an individual is never left alone, and a group is involved in all the segments of his life, indoctrination, change of diet, sense of guilt and fear, etc.
The following are some of the most dangerous and destructive religious movements in the World:

Satanism

As the name says itself- Satanism is categorized as a religion of the worshippers of Satan. Public practice od Satanism began in 1966 with the American occultist Anton Szandor LaVey who wrote a book called Satanic Bible. This religion rejects the existence of any form of supernatural beings, basing itself on atheistic and materialistic beliefs. Some of the satanic sects are well known for their destructive activities such as the "Beasts of Satan" whose members committed murders in Italy between 1998- 2004, or the Order of Nine Angels, the group from the 1960s that affirmed human sacrifice.

Peoples Temple

This religious movement was founded in 1955 by Jim Jones. Jim Jones promoted a message which was a combination of Christianity and social politics with an accent on the racial equality, which is, to be honest, not a destructive system of beliefs. However, this movement is mostly known for the murders of Congressman Leo Ryan and members of his delegation, after which John convinced the members to commit suicide. November 18, 1978, will be known as greatest single loss of American civilian life after 909 people, members of Temple, committed suicide.

Heaven's Gate

Marshall Applewhite, a founder of the cult Heaven's Gate, believed he was a descendant of Jesus Christ. He spread a message among his followers that the world is going to be ruined by aliens and that all of them should leave the earth before this happen. The idea was a massive suicide that would provide their souls a journey with Comet Hale- Bopp, which was believed to be a spaceship. Members of this group took phenobarbital mixed with pineapple and vodka to commit suicide.

Church of Euthanasia

This group believes that the world is overpopulated. They actually encourage its members to take action such as taking one's life, avoiding procreation at all costs, as well as promoting cannibalism to avoid burying the bodies of the dead. Because of their strange practices and beliefs, this church came under fire many times by police. This Church asks from people to kill themselves in order to save the planet. One of their most unpopular videos was the video "I Like to Watch" which showed 9/ 11 footage side-by-side with hardcore porn.

Aum Shinrikyo

A religious movement founded by Shoko Asahara, the Japanese man who claimed to be "the Lamb of God." He claimed he could cleanse members of his group of all the sins and help them survive the End of the world. This group released sarin on the three lines of the Tokyo subway during the rush hour causing the death of 12 people, severely injuring 50 and causing temporary injuries to thousands.

Parody Religions / Some Of The World's Funniest Religions

Parody religions are mostly the system of beliefs that mock the spiritual convictions of others. The accent of most of these religions is having fun through humor, satire or burlesque. Some of the most popular parody religions are:

Invisible Pink Unicorn

This religion was created as a parody of theistic and their definitions of the God. The basic idea of Invisible Pink Unicorn's members is to discuss and argue about supernatural beliefs which they compare with Russell's cosmic teapot.

The Worst Religion Ever

This religion was created in honor to Ed Wood who was known as a director of cheap films in the 1940s. Ed Wood was famous for his constant revisions on the set and directed the movie "Plan 9 From Outer Space" which was claimed to be the worst movie in the history of movie-making. Followers of the Church of the Heavenly Wood rely on a possibility to find a true path to the happiness in life by watching his films.

Pastafarianism

Parody religion Pastafarianism is known as the Church of the flying spaghetti. Even though it is a parody, this religion has a huge number of followers. The basic belief of Pastafarians is that monster in the shape of spaghetti with meatballs created the earth when he was drunk. Pastafarianism is, similar to Invisible Pink Unicorn, modern version of the Russell ` s teapot.

Dudeism

This religious movement is inspired by the movie "The Big Lebowski" and its main character "The Dude" who was a very appreciated guru. Their belief system is a modern form of Taoism, and it advocates the practice of "being cool-headed", "taking it easy" or "going with the flow". The number of Dudeist Priests is estimated on 350,000 nowadays.

Jediism

Jediism is a relatively new religious, nontheistic movement which is based on the philosophical and spiritual ideas of the depiction of the Jedi in Star Wars. Followers of Jedism movement follow the moral codes which are demonstrated by the Star Wars Jedis.

Zoroastrianism

Dating back at least 3000 years, Zoroastrianism is among the oldest religions in the world. It is still practiced to an extent in India and Iran (where it was founded), and, as with most religions in the modern day, it has small communities around the world. The religion was powerful during ancient times when it was the state religion of Persia, but today its adherents have fallen to numbering below possibly 200,000. The religion has seen some debate in the West due to its early adoption of a dualistic approach (in opposition to polytheistic) to the universe. Good and evil are two separate concepts, but they both exists to make up the whole. They exist physically in the universe but also in the mind. The opposing forces of good and evil, represented by Ahura Mazda and, Angra Mainyu respectively, form a similar dichotomy that God and Satan form in the Abrahamic religion Christianity.

Ahura Mazda is considered to perpetuate the creative force, Spenta Mainyu; Angra Mainyu is not the exact opposite of Ahura Mazda (and certainly not the same as Satan), but this entity is considered to control the destructive force opposing the creative one. Disease, sickness, and death are all consequences of Angra Mainyu's attack on Spenta Mainyu. These two forces mirror physical aspects such as life and death, light and dark, and good and evil.

Again, displaying similarities to Christianity (though founded at least a millennium earlier), God (Ahura Mazda) gifted free will to mankind, who may choose the be good or evil. If the former is pursued, everlasting happiness and peace is the reward; the latter leads to suffering in Hell. This area of the religion deals with the mind's duality, and there we can see dualities like sadness and happiness or truth and deception. Once all mankind decides to follow the path of good, then there will be a paradise on Earth, for good will have defeated evil. Overall, it is believed humanity is inherently good and gives a positive prognosis on the future of the battle between Ahura Mazda and Angra Mainyu. Interestingly, man is thus seen as an assistant rather than a servant of God, for if a man *chooses* good, he will help God defeat evil. Under this condition, all humans are considered equal (man, woman, child), and only are unequal in their level of righteousness.

The founder of the religion, Zoroaster, is also known by the name Zarathustra, which is also the main character in Nietzsche's writing, *Thus Spake Zarathustra*. He was married with children and he rejected the polytheism of his contemporaries. He also did not approve of the oppressive system in his society, hence one of the main tenets of Zoroastrianism being that all humans are equal. Around the time he was 30 (again similar to the Christian savior), Zoroaster had a vision that there was only one God worthy of worship, and he attempted to impart that to others. Initially, it is believed, he only had one person convert, and the convert was a family member. The local religious leaders did not accept his warnings against over ritualization and the local laypeople, who believed in some gods, were discontent with his reclassification of those gods as simply evil spirits doing the work of the one Evil Spirit.

By the time of the first Persian Empire, Zoroastrianism was an established religion in western Iran. The rulers, starting with Cyprus the Great, were followers of the religion. Unlike certain other empires, Cyprus did not foist the religion upon all his subjects. The subjects included the Jews who had been Babylon, and he even allowed them to return to their homeland and rebuild their Temple. Resulting from this act of good, Zoroastrian ideals heavily influenced Judaism following the return to Jerusalem.

When Alexander the Great of Macedonia arrived and conquered the Persian Empire, the religion was particularly harmed. Many of the leaders and priests were killed and the texts destroyed. However, the core tenets remained and, after Alexander died and his empire began to fragment, the religion enjoyed more freedoms in various regions. Shortly after Alexander's successors were removed from power, another set of rulers entered. They were not particularly interested in forcing religion upon their subjects and governed in a fashion reminiscent of their Zoroastrian predecessors. A centralized church was eventually set up and became rather wealthy. This afforded it independence and some insulation from other growing religions of the time, but, as with everything in history, the rulers eventually fell to another power.

In the 7th century during the Arab conquests, Persia fell under Arab rule. This conquest was more detrimental to Zoroastrianism than the attack from Alexander, but they were allowed to keep their particular religious practices provided they paid an extra tax. Life was not great for adherents, though, he also faced many laws that encouraged the conversion to Islam and social pressures to do the same. Zoroastrianism was destined to become a minority religion in the former Persian Empire. The conquests of the Turks and Khans was further harmful, and the status of the religion deteriorated even further. The ruling Khan converted to Islam instead of Zoroastrianism, effectively ensuring the religion would remain a minority religion.

Zoroastrians believe fire represents the wisdom of God, but it does not imply they worship fire. They worship God. Furthermore, because Zoroaster was against over ritualization in his time, modern Zoroastrians do not focus significantly on the rituals associated with the religion. It is a largely individualistic religion in which believers can pray how they want. They are expected to follow the three central ideals of Good Thoughts, Good Deeds, and Good Words. When praying – which is traditionally done several times a day but the frequency is up to the believer – they generally face some source of light (such as the sun, fire, or, in modernity, artificial life is also permissible), so that they may face the representation of God. This is likely the reason many people who know little about the religion think they worship fire. The religion also has been known to keep sacred fires alive inside temples as a way to stay constantly connected to God.

As death is the work of evil, and nature is the work of good, the corpses of Zoroastrians should not be buried in the ground.

This mixes the impure dead body, which has been contaminated with evil death, into the sacred ground. Hence bodies used to be left on a high tower, built specifically for the funeral ritual. The bodies were left for vultures to eat and the sun to desiccate. This has the added benefit of exposing the body to constant good during the day (the sun). The practice, however, is often impractical in modern societies as there are laws about simply leaving decaying corpses out in the open. In India, there is still an area with the Towers of Silence, where a large portion of the extant Zoroastrian population leaves their dead. Even in India, though, the modernization of the country is forcing the remaining Zoroastrians to rethink the tradition. For those who cannot participate in such rituals due to laws or impracticability, cremation is usually the optimal choice for it turns the things associated with death such as stench and ugliness into simple ash.

Conclusion

Judging by events in human history to date, it seems likely that religion of some kind or another will continue to be practiced by the majority of the world's population, at least for the foreseeable future. However, what form this religious adherence will take is open to interpretation and debate. There can be no doubt that the story of religion around the world will have to be rewritten frequently.

Some religions are growing, whereas others are shrinking. According to the Pew Research Center for Religion and Public Life, there is currently a dynamic shift taking place in the number of people practicing the major world religions. The Center's researchers believe that if current trends continue, then by 2050 the number of Christians and Muslims will be equal, the number of Buddhists will remain approximately the same, and the number of Christians in the United States will decline from 75% to 66% of the population.

Whilst atheism, agnosticism and other forms of non-affiliation are growing in some countries, it is predicted that there will be an overall drop in the number of people who claim not to be a member of any religion. At the moment, there are thought to be around 1.1 billion people who do not identify with any particular religion. However, whilst the Pew Research Center predicts that this will increase to 1.2 billion by 2050, this will not keep pace with the global population growth as a whole. Currently, the non-affiliated make up 16% of the world's population, but by 2050 this figure is predicted to settle at 13%. This change can largely be attributed to the fact that birth rates among the countries and classes that ascribe to these nonreligious ways of life are lower than the replacement rate, while the population is expected to grow, or even explode, for other areas that tend to be religious. The continual spread of knowledge and the fact that many religions are not compatible with each other may reverse this downward trend for the nonreligious; however, birth rates and population statistics cannot be ignored.

The ways in which future generations practice and follow any particular religion is impossible to predict with any degree of certainty, but understanding our cultural past as a species is important to understanding how we arrived at our current understanding of the world and how we approach the meaning of life itself. Religion and spirituality will, therefore, be an ongoing area of study for many years to come. It will also continue to play a role in global politics, especially if the world population in places with diverging religions continues to grow. Regardless of differences, we are all still human, and we can see commonalities between religions and indeed cultures. The study of religion should help you better understand those around you who are different.

CPSIA information can be obtained
at www.ICGtesting.com
Printed in the USA
BVOW10s0640111217
502481BV00013BA/489/P